My Low Carb

Caribbean Cuisine

By: Kayanna D. Jennings

Dedications

This book is dedicated to seven special people in my life. These seven people have impacted my life in such an amazing way.

Edward, I want to thank you for always pushing me to go after my dreams. You encouraged me from the day I met you to write because you knew writing was my passion. Thank you for inspiring me everyday to be the best person I can be. Love you Always.

Grandma, I miss you more and more every day. You really inspired me to write most of these recipes in this book. A lot of these recipes I watched you cook them growing up. I wish you could be here to see this book being published. I love you and miss you. Rest in Peace Grandma.

Vinity, another loved one gone to soon. I told you I was adding you to the acknowledgments of my first book but ended up taking the acknowledgment section out because it was too long. You didn't get a chance to read my first book but I know you would have been proud. Thank you for teaching me how to be a strong woman. Thank you for never judging me but most importantly thank you for building my confidence. I will never forget you. I love You Always. Rest in Peace Nitty.

Tiffany, Growing up we were always close and it hurts me every day that you are no longer here. I can't call you; I can't see you and I can't hear your unique and one of a kind laugh. I wish before you left this earth; you would have taught me how to make rice. I swear you made the best rice and Oxtails. I love you always "Taye Loso… In Case You Didn't Know So"! Like you would say ☺ Rest in Peace baby girl.

Tacari and Tyrese; my two baby brothers. I love you two dearly.

To my favorite cousin; Bianca. I love you as if you were my sister. I can talk to you about anything and your always willing to listen. You are the sweetest person I know. Love you always.

Table of Contents

MY LOW CARB
CARIBBEAN
CUISINE

KAYANNA D. JENNINGS

My Story

I want to start off by saying, thank you for purchasing my second book. In case you have not purchased my first book. My name is Kayanna D. Jennings and I am the author of "My Low Carb Journal" and the creator of "mylowcarbcaribbeancuisine.com". I have been eating low carb on and off for five years. When I started eating Low Carb I was 247 pounds. Within the course of a few months, I had lost over 60 + pounds following Atkins Induction. Then I faced some personal issues and adapted back to unhealthy eating habits. I gained most of the weight I lost back. So, I began eating low carb again and have just recently gotten back to the size I was when I first lost weight. I am still on a journey to becoming the "best me that I can be". And even though I am not exactly where I want to be, I am proud of myself for losing all of that weight. During my journey I learned when I am consistent with eating the low carb way, I lose weight effortlessly. I feel better, have more energy and am better overall but once I start falling off the wagon everything begins going downhill from there. Most people would ask, why haven`t you stayed consistent and remain low carb? My answer to that would be my lack of understanding in the past, that low carb eating isn't a diet but more of a lifestyle. You see, up until about a year ago I didn't realize that all I had to do was take the food I love eating and modify it the low carb way. Once I realized this, eating low carb has been so easy and very enjoyable.

I grew up in a West Indian household, I ate things like Stew Peas, Curry Goat, Oxtails, Festival, Rice and Peas, Saltfish Fritters, Fried Dumpling and so much more. During the beginning of my low carb journey I missed eating these things but I don't have to miss them anymore; because I make them the low carb way. And while modifying these recipes I grew up eating. I was inspired to create this book to help those who have never had Caribbean Food and would love to try new and exciting meals while eating low carb. As well as those who have had the pleasure of eating Caribbean Food and just want to continue eating them. These recipes come from Jamaica, Barbados, Trinidad, Aruba, Bahamas, Haiti and other Islands in The Caribbean. It has been said that, The Caribbean is known for having flavorful dishes that are packed with amazing herbs and spices. We are very big on eating a lot of stews and you will noticed that while reading this book but we also enjoy sweet treats like Easter Bun, Cassava Balls and Kurma. As well as, delicious beverages like: Peanut Punch, Sorrel and Ginger Beer.

Some of these recipes may be a bit higher in carbs for those following the Atkins Induction Phase. But you will be pleasantly surprised to know that many of these recipes are under 20 net carbs and are Atkins Induction Friendly. If you are following any particular low carb program, just make sure whatever recipe you use fits into your carb count. If you have absolutely no idea what

"Atkins Induction is or what net carbs are. I will explain what they are and mean in the "FAQ" section of this book. Thank you once again for purchasing my book and I hope you enjoy these recipes.

Why Should I Start Living A Low Carb Lifestyle?

Why should I start living a low carb lifestyle? And I answer that question by saying why wouldn't you want to be able to stabilize your insulin? So you don't have a carb coma like you experience when you eat a big bowl of spaghetti; and instantly feel tired and sluggish? Why wouldn't you want to lower your blood pressure so you're no longer at risk of a heart attack? Why wouldn't you want to lose and maintain the weight you have lost? Why wouldn't you want to feel fuller after eating a low carb meal? Because protein makes you feel fuller faster and longer. Why wouldn't you want to increase the good cholesterol and decrease the bad cholesterol? Yes, there is good and bad cholesterol that not even our doctors talk to us about. Please open up your minds to the great benefits of following a low carb diet.

What are carbs? How do they work? Why should I restrict them?

Carbs (carbohydrates) provide fuel. They give us the energy we need every day to perform our daily duties. So carbs are actually good for you. So I know your saying to yourself. Well if they give you energy then how can they be bad for you? I'll answer that for you. All carbs are not created equally. And because of this it is best to avoid high consumption of the wrong ones called: Simple Carbs; which can often lead to weight gain. Think of carbs like the gas you need to keep your car running. Let's say you're filling up your car with gas but you try to put more gas than your car needs. The gas will automatically begin to spill because it has nowhere else to go because it is already filled. That is kind of what happens when you eat too many Simple Carbs. Well it doesn`t spill but it finds somewhere else to go. After you eat a meal high in Simple Carbs, it is converted into sugar called (Glucose). The Glucose enters your bloodstream and your Pancreas begins to secrete Insulin. Then your body begins storing what it needs from it to your Muscles and Liver. If these parts of the body are already full with Glycogen; which is a storing kind of carbohydrate. Your body stores whatever is left over as body fat. And that is why it is very important to eliminate most Simple Carbs from our diets as much as possible. And then replace them with more Complex Carbs and Fiber.

If carbs provide me with fuel to get through the day and I'm eating low carb. Where will I get fuel from then?

Good question! Remember we are eating low carb. Not "no carbs". So you will still eat carbs but you will eat carbs from vegetables and you will be surprised to know there are carbs in other things you are allowed to eat like cheese, heavy cream, some condiments and many more. And since your body won't be getting the normal high quantity of carbs it is used to getting. It will go into a state called "Ketosis"; which is when the body is using fat for energy. But that does not mean you will be feeding your body donuts, cakes and muffins (unless their low carb approved and even then you have to eat them in moderation). But, you will be feeding your body fats like: Avocados, Grass-fed Butter, MCT Oil, Coconut Oil, chicken thigh, fatty cuts of steak and you can even enjoy the skin of the chicken. And not only will our bodies be using the fat we eat for energy but it will use our stored body fat as well. This also means the more fat you eat; the faster you lose weight. At first you may feel a bit tired because your body isn't used to this form of eating and has to adapt but I promise you that within a few days. You will experience this burst of energy. You never had before and will embark upon a different way of eating. On a typical low carb day you may enjoy eggs for breakfast, with bacon and you can enjoy coffee with some heavy cream but no sugar. You can use Splenda or Stevia to sweeten it though. For lunch you will enjoy a spinach salad with berries (because their low in carbs and sugar). For a mid-day snack you will enjoy nuts and make shakes out of them. And finally for dinner you will enjoy a nice juicy steak covered with butter, because butter has a lot of fat in it. And as a side dish you will eat some steamed broccoli and wash this down with some water because you need plenty of water to function and maintain a healthy weight. Those meals I listed are just a few of the many low carb meals you can enjoy daily but don't expect those typical meals to be in this book because this book is based on Caribbean dishes. But you can expect them to all be low in carbs.

Why does low carb get a bad rap?

Low carb gets a bad rap because people hear low carb and they believe it means you eat no carbs. And this I find to be absolutely hilarious because we live in a world where no one educates themselves anymore. Too quick to actually try things and see if it actually benefits you. Low carb is not a no carb diet, and it definitely isn't an excuse to eat so much protein that your kidneys no longer can function properly. Low carb is: low carbs, high fat (healthy fats) and moderate protein. And like I stated before, low carbs means focusing on eating lots of green leafy veggies and berries. Healthy fats such as avocados and coconut oil. Protein like: chicken thighs and juicy steaks. And if you have a sweet tooth, you can enjoy cakes, pies, ice cream, donuts and so much more; as long as you modify these treats the low carb way. And I promise you once you realize that you can still enjoy everything you grew up eating and still eat the low carb way. You will say to yourself: "why didn`t I do this sooner?" So don't believe the hype. There are people who criticize everything that they are unsure of.

What is this Atkins Induction thing you keep speaking of?

Atkins Induction is Phase 1 of the "Atkins Diet Plan". During this Phase, you consume no more than 20 net carbs from a list of "Acceptable Food". The list of food consist of vegetables, cheeses, meats, fats, spices, herbs, creams and oils that are low in carbs. This phase last two weeks and then you move onto the next phase (you can follow Induction longer than two weeks if you want). When you move onto the next phase after Induction, you add more carbs back into your diet. As you get closer to your goal you move to the next phase and then finally go into Maintenance. The Atkins protocol is very similar to most Low Carb diets out there.

What are net carbs?

Net Carbs are the calculation of Carbohydrates minus Fiber and Sugar Alcohol (if there is any) in food. For example: If a slice of Almond Bread has 6 grams of carbs and has 4 grams of fiber. You would simply do this subtraction as follows: 6-4= 2. So that slice of bread has 2 net carbs. When counting carbs, this calculation is very important. It helps you keep an accurate track of how many carbs your consuming daily.

Is there any way I can get a more descriptive explanation on how low

carb works?

Yes, once again you can purchase my first (very short and straight to the point) book "My Low Carb Journal"; where I explain everything you need to know about "Low Carb". My book provides tips, FAQ, meal ideas and a food list of foods you can and should eat.

How can I contact you if I have any questions and concerns?

My Contact Info Is Listed Below:

My Website: www.mylowcarbcaribbeancuisine.com

Facebook: www.facebook.com/mylowcarbcaribbeancuisine

Instagram: instagram.com/ mylowcarbcaribbeancuisine

Pinterest: http://www.pinterest.com/Mylowcarbcaribb/

Gmail: Kayannadeejennings@gmail.com

Unfamiliar Items:

There may be many items in these recipes that you have never heard of before. I want to explain to you what they are and where you can purchase them.

Almond Blanched Flour: This is made of ground Almonds that have had the skin removed off of them. Removing the skin of the almonds and then processing them through a food processor leaves you with this finely ground flour. I recommend using Almond Blanched Flour because it works great with cakes, pies, pancakes and other pastries. You should never mistake Almond Meal for Almond Blanched Flour. Almond Meal is ground Almonds that still has the skin. It is does not have the same fine texture as Almond Blanched Flour and does not taste as good. Almond Flour is also very low in carbs. ¼ Cup of Almond flour is about 3 Net Carbs.

Purchase Almond Blanched Flour at Amazon.com, Netrition.com, Shop.honeyville.com, Trader Joe`s and most organic stores.

Coconut Flour: Is dried coconuts that has been processed. It is also very high in fiber. Unlike Almond Flour, Coconut Flour is more trickier to bake and cook with. A little goes a long way with coconut flour. If a recipe normally calls for 1 cup of regular flour; you would need to decrease the amount of coconut flour you're using. For this reasons you won't find too many recipes in this book with coconut flour. But in my personal opinion it is easier to disguise the taste of coconut in coconut flour when paired with the right ingredients than it is for Almond Flour. Coconut flour and Almond flour both have their advantages and disadvantages.

Purchase Coconut Flour at Amazon.com, Netrition.com, Bobsredmills.com, Trader Joes and most organic stores.

Dixie Diner Carb Counters All Purpose Low Carb Flour: This is one of the best tasting low carb flours I have ever tried. It is amazing how much this flour taste and resembles regular flour in appearance. It has only 2 net carbs and 1 gram of sugar.

Purchase Dixie Diner`s Club All Purpose Flour at Dixiediner.com, Amazon.com and Netrition.com.

Whole Psyllium Husk: This is a fiber often used to relieve constipation. It also adds a nice texture and taste to many baked goods. Without it I honestly don't know how a lot of my recipes would taste. It really is a great addition.

Purchase Psyllium Husk at Amazon.com, Netrition.com, Vitaminshoppe.com, Trader Joe`s and most organic stores.

Miracle Noodles: These are made from a dietary fiber called Glucomannan. They slow down digestion and keep you full for a long period of time. They are also very low in carbs (about 1 net carb). They also go well with any pasta dish you can think of because they take on the flavor of whatever sauce you put them in.

Purchase Miracle Noodles at Miraclenoodle.com, Amazon.com, Netrition.com, Vitacost.com and most organic stores.

Ciao Carb Nutriwell Penne Pasta: This is one of the best tasting low carb pastas I have ever tried. It is not the lowest in carbs (15 net carbs per 1 cup). But it is still lower in carbs compared to most pasta noodles on the market. It is also packed with fiber and protein.

Purchase Ciao Carb Nutriwell Penne Pasta at Netrition.com

Explore Asian Organic Soybean Spaghetti Noodles: This is a noodle made out of soybean. It is low in carbs, (6 net carbs per 2oz.) and high in protein.

Purchase Explore Asian Organic Soybean Spaghetti Noodles at Netrition.com, Vitacost.com and Amazon.com

Bonus: You will notice a lot of these recipes called for Scallions and Sprigs Thyme. My suggestion to you is if the recipe does not call for scallions that are chopped in small pieces. After you are done cooking, remove the scallion unless you want to eat it. Some people do and others don't. The same thing applies for Sprig Thyme. I doubt you would want to eat anything other than the actually thyme.

Safety Tip: Always wash and soak raw meat in cold water with lime juice or vinegar to get rid of any germs. Make sure after you place your meat in lime juice or vinegar; you wash it again a few times in plain cold water.

Cauliflower White Rice

Yield: 8 Servings

Ingredients:

1 Head of Cauliflower (Large)

1 Tablespoon Unsalted Butter

1/2 Tablespoon Salt

1/2 Teaspoon Black Pepper

1 Tablespoon Olive Oil

1 Teaspoon Dried Thyme (Optional)

Food Processor

Instructions:

Begin by washing the Cauliflower thoroughly and pat dry. Remove the green core of the cauliflower and discard it. With a big knife, begin chopping the cauliflower florets into small pieces. They should be small enough so you can place a good amount of the florets into your food processor. Once everything is chopped; place the florets into your food processor. Pulse until the pieces are small. Make sure not to pulse it too long. In my processor it takes about 5 seconds to get the size I want and my food processor isn't the best. A good way to know the pieces are perfect is the pieces should resemble the size of regular rice. Scoop the cauliflower rice out and turn your stove on medium low heat. Put the olive oil in the pan. Allow it to heat up a bit. Then place the cauliflower rice, salt, thyme black pepper and butter in the pan. Allow it to cook for about 8 minutes. With a big spoon, keep stirring the rice, so it doesn't stick to the pan.

Suggestion: *Cauliflower white rice can be used as an alternative to regular white rice. It goes well with Curry Goat, Oxtails, Brown Stew Chicken and Escovitch Fish.*

Approx. Nutritional Facts per Serving: *55.9 Calories, 3.4g Fat, 3.2g Net Carbs, 2.2g Protein*

Cauliflower Rice and Peas

Yield: 10- 12 Servings

Ingredients:

1 Head of Cauliflower Rice (Large/Use the same technique from the cauliflower white rice recipe)

1 Can Kidney Beans

¾ Cup Coconut Milk

2 Garlic Cloves Finely (Chopped)

1 Tablespoon Unsalted Butter

2 Scallions

1 Teaspoon Dried Thyme

1/2 Tablespoon Salt

1/2 Teaspoon Black Pepper

2 Tablespoons Olive Oil

Food Processor

Instructions:

Follow the same exact instructions that are listed for the cauliflower white rice recipe. Once you have finished running the cauliflower through the food processor. Turn your stove on medium low heat. Add the olive oil to the pan, then add the garlic and begin stirring the garlic. Don't allow it to burn. Once the garlic has a little color; add the cauliflower rice and cook it for about 6 minutes. You want to keep stirring the cauliflower rice during this time. At this point add the coconut milk, thyme, beans, scallion, butter, salt and black pepper. Mix everything together. Cover with a lid slightly at this time for another 5 minutes or until the cauliflower is as soft as you would like it to be.

(Once you're ready to serve the rice, remove the Scallion)

Suggestion: *Cauliflower Rice and Peas is best with Oxtails, Brown Stew Chicken and Escovitch Fish*

Approx. Nutritional Facts per Serving: *96.1 Calories, 4.6g Fat, 8.0g Net Carbs, 4.6g Protein*

Pumpkin Balls (Inspired by Cassava Balls)

Yield: 6 Servings

Ingredients:

1 Can of Pumpkin Puree/Mashed (Look for a can that has no added sugar)

If you cannot find one, you can buy a regular pumpkin and puree it as well

6 Boiled Eggs

2 Eggs for wet wash

5 Cups of water

Pinch of Salt

Pinch of Black Pepper

1 Cup Almond Blanched Flour

3 Tablespoons Splenda

2 to 3 Cups Canola oil

Thin dish Towel

Fact:

Cassava Balls are normally made using Cassava but Cassava is very high in carbs. So the Pumpkin still works well in this recipe and it happens to be low in carbs. The Splenda helps give the pumpkin a bit of sweetness that Cassava has. You don't have to use Splenda. You can always substitute the Splenda for Stevia.

Instructions:

Place the Pumpkin Puree in a thin dish towel. Tie the towel up and begin to squeeze all the extra moisture out. You need to squeeze as much of the moisture as you can. If there is too much moisture it will make it hard for the pumpkin to stay on the boiled eggs. Once all the moisture is out. Put the Pumpkin in a big bowl and place it in the fridge. Grab a pot with the eggs and fill it up with about 5 cups of water. Turn the stove on medium high heat. Boil the 6 eggs for 10 minutes or more (depending on your stove). Once the eggs are done boiling; take them out carefully and place them in a bowl with cold water. And let them sit for 15 minutes. Once the eggs are cool, take them out, and remove the shell of the egg. Take the pumpkin out of the fridge as well. With a fork, begin mashing the puree to make sure all the lumps are gone. Add the salt, pepper and splenda to the pumpkin. Mix everything with your fork so everything is evenly distributed. Grab a plate and begin making the balls. Take about a small hand full of the pumpkin mixture and form a ball. Flatten the ball and then place the egg in the center of the ball. Then begin shaping the pumpkin mixture all around the egg. So it is covering the entire egg. You should not see any of the egg. If you discover that the pumpkin can't cover the whole egg with the amount of pumpkin you scooped out. Then just simply scoop out more of the pumpkin to cover the rest of the egg. Place each ball on a plate and continue the steps. Then grab a bowl, beat the two eggs for a wet wash. In another bowl, add the Almond Flour. Now coat the pumpkin balls in the egg wash and then coat it in the Almond flour. Turn your stove on to medium heat and add the canola oil. Wait about 5 minutes, to test if the oil is hot enough. Sprinkle a little almond flour in it, if it starts to sizzle. Then the oil is ready. Place the balls in the oil for 2 to 3 minutes. It should be a golden brown color. Place on paper towels.

Approx. Nutritional Facts per Serving: *255.1 Calories, 19.3g Fat, 8.g Net Carbs, 11.5g Protein*

Kurma Pork Rinds (Mithai)

Yield: 6 Servings

Ingredients:

2 oz Pork Rinds

1 Cup Water

1 Ginger Root (Mashed)

3 Tablespoons Splenda

2 Tablespoons Butter

1 Cinnamon Stick

1 Medal Bowl

1 Teaspoon Orange Extract (Optional)

Fact:

Kurma (Mithai) is a very popular treat in Trinidad and Guyana; as well as other parts of The Caribbean. It is typically made with all purpose flour and milk. The dough is flattened and cut into long pieces. Then it is fried and placed in this amazing glaze; but since this recipe is modified the low carb way. The glaze will be accompanied by Pork Rinds. If you didn't know Pork Rinds are a great low carb/ keto Snack. I added the orange extract to mine just as an experiment and it was great. You will be so surprised at how much this does not taste like Pork Rinds.

Instructions:

Place the Pork Rinds in the medal bowl and put it to the side. Turn your stove on medium heat and begin by putting the water in the pot. Place it on the stove. Add the butter, ginger and cinnamon stick. Using a big spoon, keep stirring the mixture until it starts to thicken. Once it begins to thicken, add the splenda. Keep stirring, don't allow it to burn! If you need to, turn down the fire. Add in the orange extract and stir for about a minute or so. Remove the ginger and cinnamon stick. Then transfer the mixture to the bowl that has the Pork Rinds in it already. With your big spoon stir the mixture and pork rinds together. So it gets evenly distributed. Eat immediately!

Approx. Nutritional Facts per Serving: *133.8 Calories, 10.8 g fat, 1.0g Net Carbs, 9.1g Protein*

Fried Dumpling

Yield: 6 Servings

Ingredients:

1 ½ Cup Dixie Diners` Club All Purpose Flour

6 Tablespoons Psyllium Husk (Whole)

½ Cup Water

½ Teaspoon Salt

1 Teaspoon Baking Powder

3 Cups Canola Oil

Instructions :

Place the flour in a big bowl, add the psyllium husk, salt, baking powder and water to the flour. With both hands begin working the dough. Your goal is to turn the entire mixture into one big ball. The dough should not be too sticky. Once you form a big ball. Put a piece of paper towel over the bowl or plate, put it to the side. Turn the stove on medium heat and pour the oil into a pot. Allow the oil to get hot; it should take about 5 minutes. While the oil is getting hot. Go back to your dough. Break off medium size pieces from the flour (about the size of a meatball). Using your hands roll the dough like you would when creating a meatball but flatten it a little bit. A good way to form a perfect ball; is to take both hands and rub them together with the dough inside in a circular motion. Place that ball on a separate plate and repeat until all the dough is finished. Now, test the oil by dropping a tiny amount of the flour in the oil. If the oil starts to sizzle; it is ready. Place each ball in the oil. Allow it to cook for about 3 to 5 minutes on each side. The balls should be a golden brown color. Place on paper towels.

Suggestion: *Fried Dumplings can go with any meat dish.*

Approx. Nutritional Facts per Serving: *126.7 Calories, 2.5 g Fat, 3.5g Net Carbs,13.0g Protein*

Festival

Yield: 6 Servings

Ingredients:

1 ½ Cup Dixie Diners` Club All Purpose Flour

6 Tablespoons Psyllium Husk (Whole)

½ Cup Water

½ Teaspoon Salt

1 Teaspoon Baking Powder

¼ Cup Splenda

5 Cups Canola Oil

Instructions :

This recipe is very similar to the recipe for Fried Dumpling but there are a few changes. Place the flour in a big bowl; add the psyllium husk, salt, baking powder, splenda and water to the flour. With both hands begin working the dough. Your goal is to form the entire mixture into one big ball. The dough should not be too sticky. It should be semi dry. Once you form a big ball. Put a piece of paper towel over a bowl or plate, put it to the side. Turn the stove on medium heat and pour the oil into a pot. Allow the oil to get hot; it should take about 5 to 7 minutes. While the oil is getting hot. Go back to your dough. Break off medium size pieces from the flour (about the size of a meatball). Using your hands roll the dough into the shape of a thick but short Hotdog. A good way to form a festival; is to take both hands and rub them together with the dough inside and as you're rubbing your hands together, the dough should start getting longer in length but remember you`re trying to create a thick hot dog like shape. Place that festival on a separate plate and repeat until all the dough is finished. Now, test the oil by dropping a small amount of flour in the oil. If the oil starts to sizzle; it is ready. Place each festival in the oil. Allow it to cook for about 3 to 5 minutes on each side. The festivals should be a golden brown color. Place on paper towels.

Suggestion: *Festivals go great with any meat dish.*

Approx. Nutritional Facts per Serving: *126.7 Calories, 2.5g Fat, 4.7 Net Carbs, 3.0 Protein*

Coleslaw

Yield: 6 Servings

Ingredients:

4 Cups Green Cabbage (Shredded)

1 Cups Purple Cabbage (Shredded)

2 Tablespoons Olive Oil

2 Tablespoons Apple Cider Vinegar

1 Teaspoon Dijon Mustard

3 Tablespoons Splenda

1 Teaspoon Salt

1 Teaspoon Black Pepper

½ Cup Purple Onion (Finely Chopped)

½ Cup Mayonnaise

¼ Cup Carrots (Chopped) (they are higher in carbs, you don't have to add it)

1 Teaspoon Dried Thyme

Instructions:

In a large size bowl, add the oil, vinegar, mustard, splenda, salt, black pepper, onion, mayonnaise, carrots and thyme together. With a fork, begin mixing everything. Add the cabbage. At this point begin mixing everything so it is evenly distributed. Put the coleslaw in the fridge for at least 15 minutes before serving.

Approx. Nutritional Facts per Serving (Carrots Included): 194.3 Calories, 17.9g Fat, 6.9g Net Carbs, 1.1g Protein

Macaroni Pie

Yield: 10 Servings

Ingredients:

2 Bags of Miracle Ziti Noodles

1 Tablespoon Butter (Melted)

3 Cups Cheddar Cheese (You can use more than one kind of cheese)

2 Eggs Whisked

1 Teaspoon Black Pepper

½ Teaspoon Salt

1 Cup Heavy Cream

Baking Pan

Extra Tablespoon Butter to grease the sides of the pan

Instructions:

Preheat oven to 350. Take the noodles out of the bag. Put them in a strainer. Run them through cold water about 3 to 4 times. The noodles will have a fishy smell and you want to get rid of that smell. Pat the noodles dry and put it to the side. In a medium size bowl, add the eggs (whisked) black pepper, salt, cream, butter and only 2 cups of the cheese. Begin to mix everything evenly with a fork. Take the mixture and pour it onto the noodles. With the same fork, mix everything. Make sure everything is evenly distributed. Then start greasing the sides of your baking pan with the extra butter. Pour the mixture onto the baking pan. With the cup of cheese you have left over. Pour the rest on top. Make sure it covers everything. Put a piece of foil paper on top of the pan (a piece that is big enough to cover the pan). Allow it to cook for 30- 45 minutes; depending on your stove. At the last 10 minutes of cooking time; remove the foil paper. So the top of the macaroni can turn a golden brown color. Let the macaroni sit for about an hour, before you cut into it.

Approx. Nutritional Facts per Serving: 284.2 Calories, 29.6g Fat, 2.3g Net Carbs, 16.4 g Protein

Baigan Choka

Yield: 6 Servings

Ingredients:

1 Large Eggplant

1 Teaspoon Salt

3 Tablespoons Coconut Oil

¼ cup Onion Sliced

2 Garlic Cloves (Chopped)

1 Scotch Bonnet Pepper (Chopped)

Instructions:

Preheat oven to 400, cut off ends of the eggplant and discard them. With a sharp knife, start poking holes/slits into the eggplant. About 8 or 10, then place on a baking pan or rack and put it in the oven for 30 minutes. After 30 minutes, take it out the oven. Let it cool for about 10 to 15 minutes. Then turn your stove on medium heat. Place your cooking pan on the stove. Add the coconut oil and onions. Let the onion cook for about 3 minutes. Go back to the eggplant, with the same knife as before. Cut through the eggplant, until you can see the inside. Now with a fork, start scrapping the inside of the eggplant onto the pan with the onion cooking. Then add salt, garlic and the chopped scotch bonnet pepper. Mix everything together. Allow this to cook for another 3 minutes.

Suggestion: *This can be served with any meat dish as a side.*

Approx. Nutritional Facts per Serving: *94.6 Calories, 7.7g Fat, 4.5 Net Carbs, 1.2g Protein*

Saltfish Fritters

Yield: About 10 Small Fritters

Ingredients:

10 oz. Saltfish (Codfish/ Soak Overnight)

2 Cups Dixie Carb Counters All Purpose Low Carb Flour

2 Cups Water

4 Eggs Whisked

1 Teaspoon Baking Powder

1 Teaspoon Black Pepper

1 Stalk Scallion (Green Onion/Chopped)

1 Scotch Bonnet Pepper (Chopped)

2 Garlic Cloves (Chopped)

½ Medium Onion (Chopped)

2 Cups Olive oil

1 Tablespoon Dried Thyme

Paper Towels

1 Tablespoon Sugar Free Ketchup

Instructions:

When buying codfish for the fritters. Make sure you buy the boneless ones. Codfish is very salty so you need to let it soak in 2-3 cups of cold water overnight. If you can, change the water every few hours. Drain and break the codfish into small pieces. In a large bowl add the cod fish, flour, water, baking powder, black pepper, scallion, scotch bonnet pepper, garlic, onion, ketchup eggs and thyme. Begin stirring everything so it is mixed evenly. Turn your stove to medium heat. Place the pan on the stove with the oil and allow it to get hot. You can test if the oil is hot by placing a small piece of the batter in the oil. If it sizzles, it is ready. With a big spoon, place a spoonful of the batter in the pan. Don't put too many fritters in the oil at one time. It will look as if the fritter isn't holding together but it is. Allow it to fry on each side for about 3 minutes. It is a good idea to place these fritters on a cooling rack because they are very oily. You can also place them on top of paper towels and then place a few paper towels on top of them and press down a bit to release some of the oil. I noticed the following day they were less oily.

Approx. Nutritional Facts per Serving: *224.1 Calories, 16.3g Fat, 3.4 Net Carbs, 13.3g Protein*

Red Pea Soup

Yield: 8 Servings

Ingredients:

2 Cups Kidney Beans (From the bag or canned)

6 to 10 Cups of Water

2 Medium Onions (Chopped)

2 Scallions

1 Scotch Bonnet Pepper

1/2 Tablespoon Salt

1 Teaspoon Black Pepper

10 oz Stew Beef

2 Sprigs Thyme

2 Garlic Cloves Mashed

Instructions:

If you are using the dry kidney beans you have to soak them in a large pot filled with lots of water overnight. But before you soak them, make sure you wash them with warm water. You can use the can kidney beans as well. Once you're ready to cook the soup. Add the Kidney beans and stew beef to the same pot of water you soaked them in overnight. Bring it to a boil for about 60 minutes on medium heat. Every 15 minutes or so, check to see if you see the water is dissolving too fast. Add more water to the pot if it is. You will probably have to add about a cup of water maybe once or twice. When the meat is tender, add the onions, scallion, scotch bonnet pepper, salt, black pepper, garlic, allspice and thyme. Also add another cup of water if needed. Lower the fire a bit and let this cook for another 20 to 30 minutes. The soup should be thick; this should not be a watery soup.

Approx. Nutritional Facts per Serving: *124.9 Calories, 2.8g Fat, 9.5g Net Carbs, 10.8 g Protein*

Chicken Back Soup

Yield: 8 Servings

Ingredients:

10 Chicken Backs

6 Chicken Drumsticks

8 Chicken Feet (Optional but Traditional)

6-8 Cups Water

2 Cups Pumpkins Diced

1 Cup Summer Squash Diced

3 Celery Sticks (Chopped)

2 Cups Onion (Chopped)

2 Scallions

1 Cup Green Bell Peppers

1 Teaspoon Allspice

1 Teaspoon Salt (more or less)

1 Teaspoon Black Pepper

1 Scotch Bonnet Pepper

3 Sprigs Thyme

3 Cups Low Carb Chicken Broth (Make sure it is no more than 1g of Carb and no added Sugar)

Fact:

This soup is normally called "Chicken Foot Soup" but I personally don't eat chicken feet but if you are an open minded person when it comes to food, then try this soup with some chicken feet. Just make sure you cut off the nails of the chicken foot and wash it thoroughly. Also, this soup is usually made with Chicken Noodle Soup Mix but it is higher in carbs so I replaced it with a chicken broth that is no more than 1g of Carbs.

Instructions:

Wash the chicken back and drumstick in 2 cups of water and 1 tbsp of lime juice. Then wash it again two times in just cold water. Make sure you really wash the meat and get rid of the lime juice you used to wash it with. Pat it dry and set it to the side. Then turn your stove on medium high heat and add the water to a large deep pot. Add the chicken pieces to the water and bring it to a boil for 15 minutes. Then after 15 minutes, add the chicken broth and allow it to cook for another 10 minutes. Then add the pumpkin, squash, celery, onion, scallion, bell peppers, allspice, salt, black pepper, scotch bonnet pepper and thyme. Turn the fire down medium low and let it cook for 45 to 60 minutes. Every 15 minutes, check the soup to see if it needs more water. Add a cup of water if needed.

Approx. Nutritional Facts per Serving: *182.2 Calories, 7.7g Fat, 6.1g Net Carbs, 19.5g Protein*

Black Bean Sauce

Yield: 6 Servings

Ingredients:

1 Bag Black Beans

About 6 Cups or More Water

2 Scallions

1 Tablespoon Parsley

3 Garlic Cloves (Mashed)

4 Thyme Sprigs

1 Cup Coconut Milk

1 Tablespoon Butter

1 Scotch Bonnet Pepper

1 Tablespoon Salt

1 Teaspoon Black Pepper

2 Pieces Turkey Neck or ham

Food Processor

Instructions:

Rinse and wash the beans. Soak them overnight in 2 cups of water in a pot. The next day, turn the stove on medium low heat. Add the pot with the beans to the stove. Add 4 cups of water and the turkey necks to the pot as well. Allow this to cook for 1 ½ hour or until the beans are soft. Every 20 to 30 minutes. Check on the beans to see if they need more water. Then take the turkey necks out of the pot and place it in a bowl. Grab a strainer and place it over a large bowl. Begin pouring the bean mixture onto the strainer. Keep about a cup of the beans that is left on the strainer and throw away the rest. In the food processor; add the bean liquid and the cup of beans you have left. Pulse until you have a smooth consistency. In the same pot you used to cook down the beans. Add the butter to the pot and place it back on the stove. Add the bean sauce you made in the food processor to the pot. Then add the parsley, garlic, thyme, coconut milk, butter, scotch bonnet pepper, salt, black pepper, scallion and turkey neck. Cook for another 45 minutes on low heat.

Approx. Nutritional Facts per Serving: *122.5 Calories, 3.3g Fat, 11.4g Net Carbs, 6.7g Protein*

Coconut Bun Mug Cake

Yield: 2 Servings

Instructions:

1 Tablespoon Coconut Flour

2 Tablespoons Psyllium Husk (Whole)

¼ Teaspoon Baking Powder

1 Tablespoon Butter (Softened)

Pinch of Salt

1 Egg (whisked)

3 Tablespoon Unsweetened Almond Milk

2 Teaspoon Almond Extract

1 Tablespoon of Coconut Flakes (finely grated)

Medium Size Mug Cup

3 Tablespoons Splenda

Instructions:

Add all the ingredients into your mug. You want a mug that is big enough to mix everything in. After you add everything; with a fork. Mix everything to make sure the mixture is evenly distributed. Place it in the microwave for 1:50 minutes. You may need to leave it in for 2 minutes. It all depends on your microwave. Take it out the microwave. Let it cool for 5 minutes. Then grab a plate. Place the plate on top of the mug. Flip the mug over and the mug cake should slide right out the mug. You can also pour some whipping cream on top of your mug cake, like I did.

Approx. Nutritional Facts per Serving: *139.5 Calories, 10.1g Fat, 6.0 Net Carbs, 3.8g, Protein*

Easter Bun

Yield: 10 Servings

Ingredients:

1 ½ Cup Almond Blanched Flour

6 Tablespoons Pysllium Husk (whole)

1 ½ Teaspoon Baking Powder

1 Teaspoon Baking Soda

½ Teaspoon Salt

¾ Cup Unsweetened Almond Milk

1 Teaspoon Cinnamon

½ Teaspoon Nutmeg

1 Teaspoon Olive Oil

1 Teaspoon Black Strap Molasses (Optional)

1 Teaspoon Dark Rum Extract

3 Large Eggs

½ Cup Butter Softened

1 Cup Splenda

1 Teaspoon Vanilla Extract

1 Teaspoon Anise Seed Extract

2 Tablespoon Strawberry Sauce (Sugar free store bought strawberry jelly)

1 Teaspoon Allspice

¼ Cup Raisins (Raisins are higher in carbs, so if you can't afford the carbs replace it with blueberries)

1 Teaspoon Lime Juice

Extra Tablespoon Butter (for greasing the pan)

Baking Pan

Fact:

Jamaican Easter Bun is traditionally eaten on Easter Sunday. Along with Escovitch Fish; it is usually accompanied with cheese. It can be eaten like a sandwich with the cheese in the middle or it can be eaten alone. When baking Easter Bun it is best to bake it in a deep square baking pan to get the best slices.

Instructions:

Preheat oven to 350. Place all the ingredients into a large bowl (except the raisins). Mix everything together, make sure you really mix everything well. You want a lump free batter. Then add in the raisins. And mix everything together again with a big fork. Make sure to leave at least a few raisins for the top of the cake. I didn't add a lot of Raisins to this recipe because Raisins are higher in carbs. If you look at the photo below; you only see one raisin. It still tastes great without tons of raisins. Grease your baking pan with a tablespoon of butter so the bun does not stick to the baking pan. Pour the mixture into the pan and place the left over raisins on top of the bun. Put it in the oven for 40 to 60 minutes (depends on your oven). After 40 minutes, stick a toothpick in the bun, if none of the batter is on the toothpick. Your cake is done.

Approx. Nutritional Facts per Serving: *277.5 Calories, 21.9g*

Fat, 11.0 Net Carbs, 6.6g Protein

Rum Raisin Whipping Cream

Yield: 2 Servings

Ingredients:

1 Cup (Cold Heavy Cream)

3 Tablespoons Splenda

½ Teaspoon Dark Rum Extract

1 Tablespoon Vanilla Extract

A few raisins (6 to 10)

Electric Hand Mixer

Fact:

The Caribbean isn't really known for Ice Cream. And even though we are more known for our stews; we still enjoy sweets like everyone else. Rum Raisin Ice Cream is a very popular Ice Cream in the Caribbean and I wanted to recreate it the "Low Carb" way but I thought to myself how about I make it a bit different. And make it super fast to make. So I came up with this. You can whip this up in just a few minutes.

Instructions:

In a large bowl, whip the heavy cream with an electric hand mixer until stiff peaks are about to form. Then add the splenda, rum and vanilla. Beat everything until peaks form. Scoop it out onto a bowl or cup and top with the raisins.

Approx. Nutritional Facts per Serving: *93.8 Calories, 8.0g Fat, 2.2g Net Carbs, 0.1g Protein*

Aruba Macadamia Nut Mug Cake (Inspired by Aruba Cashew Nut Cake)

Yield: 2 Servings

Ingredients (Cake):

1 Tablespoon Almond Flour

1 Tablespoon Ground Macadamia

2 Tablespoons Psyllium Husk (Powder)

¼ Teaspoon Baking Powder

Pinch of Salt

1 egg

1 Teaspoon Almond Extract

5 Tablespoons Almond Milk

5 Tablespoons Splenda

1 Tablespoon Butter

Frosting:

1oz Cream Cheese

2 Tablespoons Splenda

¼ Teaspoon Almond Extract

1 Tablespoon Ground Macadamia (Used to sprinkle on top of the frosting and cake)

Food Processor

Facts:

Aruba Cashew Nut Cake is normally made using Cashews but I replaced the Cashews with Macadamias because their known as a "Low Carb Go to Nut". I also replace the Egg Whites that this cake`s frosting has with Cream Cheese because just like the Macadamia Nuts. Cream Cheese is a go to Low Carb item as well.

Instructions:

You can make your own ground Macadamia. By placing it in the food processor and letting it run through until it was a fine consistency. Place the rest of what you don't need in a zip lock bag. Then add all the ingredients together in a mug. With a fork, begin stirring everything. Making sure everything is equally distributed. Place the mug in the microwave for 2 minutes. You may need to keep it in the microwave longer. It all depends on your microwave. In a small bowl, add the cream cheese, splenda and almond extract. Mix everything together with your fork. Take the mug out of your microwave when it is done. Place a Plate over the top of the cake. Flip the cake, so the plate is now on the bottom of the mug. And the cake should slide right out. Let it cool for a bit before you put the frosting on top. Once it has cooled down a bit. Spread the frosting on top of the cake. Pour the ground macadamias on top.

Approx. Nutritional Facts per Serving (Cake): 150.7 Calories, 11.7g Fat, 6.7g Net Carbs, 1.6g Protein

Approx. Nutritional Facts per Serving (Frosting): 75.1 Calories, 7.7gFat, 2.6 Net Carbs, 1.4g Protein

Mini Caribbean Bread Pudding

Yield: Makes Two Mini Cakes/8 Servings

Ingredients (Cake):

2 Tablespoons Almond Flour

6 Tablespoons Psyllium Husk

½ Teaspoon Baking Powder

2 Tablespoons Butter

Pinch of Salt

2 egg Whisked

7 Tablespoons Unsweetened Almond Milk

2 Teaspoons Almond Extract

5 Tablespoons Splenda

Egg Mixture:

¼ Teaspoon Cinnamon

¼ Teaspoon Nutmeg

1 Tablespoon Dark Rum Extract

¼ Cup Raisins

1 Cup Almond Milk

4 Eggs

4 Tablespoons Melted Butter

1/3 Cup Splenda

Extra Tablespoon Butter

Instructions:

Begin by making the mug cake, pour all ingredients into your mug and mix everything together. Then place it in your microwave for 3 to 6 minutes. How long the mug cake takes, really depends on your microwave. You may want to open the microwave every few minutes; to see if the cake is done. You will know your cake is ready, when the batter resembles regular cake. If the cake comes out a bit hard; that is okay because when making bread pudding you`re supposed to use dry day old bread. Now onto the mixture the cake is soaked in. Grab a separate bowl whisk the eggs and then add the milk. Mix that together. Then add in the rest of the ingredients. Put it to the side. Take the extra tablespoon of butter and grease the pan you're using to bake the bread pudding. Then cut your mug cake into small cubes and place them into the pan. Now pour the wet mixture on top, and allow the cake to soak in the mixture for 15 minutes. Then place it in the oven and bake for 30 -40 minutes at 375. Check on the pudding every 10 minutes to make sure it doesn`t burn.

Approx. Nutritional Facts per Serving: 253.1 Calories, 16.2g Fat, 12.0g Net Carbs, 8.3g Protein

Pine Tarts

Yield: About Small 6-7 Tarts

Ingredients (Tart Dough):

2 Cups Blanched Almond Flour

2 Tablespoons Butter

1 Teaspoon Splenda

¼ Teaspoon Salt

Food Processor

Filling:

2 Cups Ripe Pineapple (Chopped)

½ Cup or More Water

1/8 Teaspoon Nutmeg

1/8 Teaspoon Cinnamon

3 Tablespoons Splenda

1 Tablespoon Vanilla Extract

Instructions:

Place the chopped pineapples in the food processor. Pulse until it is a smooth consistency. Turn your stove on medium low heat. Add the pineapple to a sauce pan and bring to simmer. With a big spoon, keep stirring the mixture, then add the nutmeg, cinnamon, splenda, vanilla and water. Mix everything with your big spoon. Then turn the stove down to low heat and place a lid on the pan slightly. Allow this to cook for about 30-40 minutes. Every 10 minutes, grab your big spoon and stir the mixture until it is a thick consistency. Add a little more water if you need to. Meanwhile, start making the dough. Add the almond flour, salt, butter and splenda to your food processor (I'm assuming you washed the food processor after putting the pineapple in it. Pulse until you see the flour and all the ingredients start coming together. It should only take around 30 seconds to do this. Pour the dough out of the food processor and wrap it in a plastic wrap and store it in the fridge for 30 minutes to an hour. Now when it comes to the dough I would say at this point you would need to experiment a bit. For me, when I place the dough in the fridge. It makes it hold together more and it`s easier to work with but some people feel that dough made out of almond flour is easier to work with when it`s room temperature. I don't think any of us are wrong. I think the brand of almond flour you use has a lot to do with this; as well as personal preference. While your dough is in the fridge; keep checking on your filling. Once it is done, let it cool for 15 or so minutes. When you're ready to begin making the tarts; preheat your oven to 350. Take the dough out of the fridge. Break off about 6 to 7 pieces of the dough. Form these pieces into balls. Then with your hands flatten the dough or if you're using a rolling pin. Roll out the dough. It should be the shape of a small to medium size circle. Then place about a little more than a tablespoon of the pineapple filling in the center of the dough. Then with a spoon, begin spreading it all around the dough. Grab the bottom left corner of the dough and fold it over to the middle and then fold the bottom right corner of the dough to the middle as well. And then finally fold the top over both of the two sides you just finished folding over. The best way to explain this is. Your objective is to form the dough into a triangle. Repeat these steps for each tart. Place each tart on parchment paper. You can place a piece of butter over each tart. The butter adds a nice buttery taste to the tarts; place in the oven for 20- 30 minutes or until the tarts are golden brown.

Approx. Nutritional Facts per Serving: *265.5 Calories, 20.1g Fat, 14.9 Net Carb, 8.1g Protein*

Ginger Beer

Yield: About 8-12 Cups

Ingredients:

1 Pound Ginger

8- 12 Cups of Water

1 ½ Cups Splenda

5 Whole Cloves

½ Cup Lime Juice (Fresh Preferred)

1 teaspoon Dark Rum Extract

2 Cups of Ice Cubes

Large Pitcher/Pot or Container

Food Processor

Instructions:

Wash the ginger. Begin cutting the ginger into small pieces so they can fit in the food processor. You don't have to worry about removing the skin of the ginger. Add the ginger to the food processor. You may have to run the ginger in batches depending on the size and quality of your food processor. Add about 1 cup of warm water to each batch. Then pour the mixture into a big pot or container. Add the cloves and rum extract. Leave it in the fridge overnight. This allows the flavors to enhance. Take it out the fridge. Grab a strainer and put it over your pitcher, container or pot. Pour the mixture onto the strainer. Then squeeze the rest of the juice out of the ginger with your hands. Discard what's left in the strainer. Add the lime juice, splenda and water. The amount of water you add depends on how much you like the flavor of ginger. Just know that ginger can be very strong. I suggest adding more than 8 cups of cold water because I don't like my ginger beer to be too strong. You can add more or less. Stir everything together with a big spoon. Serve over ice.

Approx. Nutritional Facts per Serving: *19.6 Calories, 0.1g Fat, 9.9 Net Carbs, 0.1g Protein*

Almond Punch (Inspired By Peanut Punch)

Yield: 2 Servings

Ingredients:

2 Tablespoons Sugar Free Almond Butter

11 oz Atkins Vanilla Shake

Pinch Nutmeg

Pinch Cinnamon

6 Ice Cubes

Facts:

This drink is inspired by the very famous Jamaican drink "Peanut Punch". It is known as an "Energy Drink". Of course it is packed with a lot of carbs so I figured out a recipe that is lower in carbs but still satisfying.

Instructions:

Add everything except the ice cubes to a blender. Pulse the ingredients for about 30 seconds. Serve over ice.

Approx. Nutritional Facts per Serving: *180.2 Calories, 13.5g Fat, 2.5g Net Carbs, 9.9g Protein*

Sorrel

Yields: About 10 or more Cups

Ingredients:

2 Cups Dried Sorrel Sepals

1 oz Ginger (Grated)

10 or more Cups of Warm Water

2 Cups Splenda

2 Tablespoons Lemon Juice

5 Pimento Seeds

1 Orange Peel

1 Teaspoon Rum Extract (Optional)

2 Cups of Ice

Instructions:

Turn the stove on medium heat. Add 6 cups water and bring it to a boil. While the water is boiling, discard the seeds in the sorrel sepals if their present. As soon as it starts to boil; take it off the fire immediately. Add the sorrel, ginger, lemon juice, pimento seeds and orange peel to the water. Let it sit overnight. Then place a large container, pitcher or pot under a strainer. Pour the sorrel mixture onto the strainer. Then add the splenda to the sorrel (liquid). Add more water, how much water? Really depends on you. It depends on how much of the sorrel flavor you like. After you add the water, add 2 cups of ice. If it is not sweet enough; add more Splenda. You can also add the rum extract add this point if you choose to.

Approx. Nutritional Facts per Serving: *11.3 Calories, 0.3g Fat, 6.8 Net Carbs, 0.6g Protein*

Kremas (Cremasse)

Ingredients:

1 Cup Almond Milk

11oz. Atkins Vanilla Shake

¼ Teaspoon Coconut Extract

½ Teaspoon Nutmeg

¼ Teaspoon Anise Star Extract

¼ Teaspoon Almond Extract

1 Teaspoon Vanilla Extract

1 Teaspoon Lime Juice

¼ Tablespoon Dark Rum Extract

1 Tablespoon Splenda

Fact:

Kremas is a popular Haitian Drink. It is normally made using evaporated milk, cream of coconut and rum.

Instructions:

Combine all the ingredients together. Place all the ingredients into a blender and allow it to blend for 30 seconds. Pour the mixture in a cup filled with ice.

Approx. Nutritional Facts per Serving: *106.3 Calories, 6.0g Fat, 1.9 g Net Carbs, 8.1g Protein*

Jamaican Style Carrot Juice

Yield: 4 or more Cups

Ingredients:

2 Pounds Carrots

3-4 Cups of Water (It may need more)

8 oz. Atkins Vanilla Shake

1 Teaspoon Nutmeg

1 Teaspoon Rum Extract (Optional)

1 Cup Splenda or more if needed

Food Processor or Blender

Instructions:

Cut the carrots in small pieces (small enough so they can fit in your blender or food processor). You may want to blend them in small batches so it can fit. With each patch you blend, add about ½ to 1 cup of water. You should let the food processor or blender run for about a minute or so. After your done running the carrots through the food processor or blender; place a strainer over a large pitcher, container or pot. Pour the carrot mixture onto the strainer. Squeeze the juice out of the carrot mixture with your hands. Squeeze as much as you can; when I say squeeze. I mean squeeze! Discard the carrot mixture that is left over. Add the vanilla shake, nutmeg and splenda to the carrot juice. You can add alittle water to the juice also. At this point, add the rum extract and mix well. Pour into a cup of ice.

Approx. Nutritional Facts per Serving: *137.6 Calories, 5.0g Fat, 9.9 g Net Carbs, 8.1g Protein*

Stew Peas

Yield: 8 Serving

Ingredients:

6 Pig Tails cut in three

1 Tablespoon Butter

1 Medium Onion (Chopped)

1 Medium Bell Pepper (Chopped)

2 Scallions

1 Scotch Bonnet Pepper

1 Tablespoon Dried Thyme

1 Teaspoon Black Pepper

1 Tablespoon Salt

1 Tablespoon Allspice

1 Cup Kidney Beans (Can or Bag)

1 Can Coconut Milk

Fact:

Stew Pea is a very popular dish in the Caribbean. Especially in Jamaica, it also happens to be my favorite Jamaican dish of all time. Stew Peas is normally made with pig tails but it can also be made with cow foot, stew beef and oxtails. Or all meats can be used together. In this recipe I am using pigtails.

Instructions:

If you are using dry beans, you need to soak them in 2 cups of water overnight. If you're using the beans in the can, you can skip that step. Since this recipe calls for pigtails, you have to soak them overnight as well. Place them in a separate pot with 3 cups of water. Once you're ready to cook the stew peas. Empty the pot of water with the pigtails and pour 6 more cups of water. Turn the stove on medium heat(for the pigtails). Then with the pot that has the peas you soaked overnight, you just add 2 more cups of water and turn your stove on low medium heat. Boil the pigtails for 2 ½ hours and the peas for 2 hours. Check on the pots to see if you need to add more water. (Note: If you are using peas that come in the can, then you can add the peas after the pigtails has boiled for two hours in the same pot).After 2 ½ hours(dried peas), transfer the peas into the pot that has the pigtails. Mix everything together. Add in the butter, onion, bell pepper, scallion, scotch bonnet pepper, thyme, black pepper, salt, allspice and coconut milk. Cook for another 45 minutes. Adjust the fire to medium low heat.

Approx Nutritional Info per Serving: *159.5 Calories, 8.8g Fat, 4.5 Net Carbs, 13.2gProtein*

Jerk Pork

Yield: 10 Servings

Ingredients:

1 ½ to 2 Pounds Pork Shoulder (Cut in chunks)

Jerk Rub:

4 to 6 Scotch Bonnet Peppers Chopped (depends on how spicy you want it, start off with a small amount first)

3 Scallions

1 Tablespoon Thyme

2 Tablespoons Ground Allspice

4 Garlic Cloves

1 Medium Onion (Chopped)

5 Tablespoons Splenda

½ Tablespoon Salt

1 Teaspoon Black Pepper

1 Teaspoon Cinnamon

1 Teaspoon Nutmeg

2 Slices Ginger Root

½ Cup Olive Oil

½ Cup Soy Sauce (Low Sodium)

1 Tablespoon Juice of a Lime

2 Tablespoons Vinegar

1 Teaspoon Browning (Optional)

¼ Cup Liquid Smoke

1 Tablespoon Sugar Free Ketchup

½ Cup Water or more

Food Processor/Blender

Instructions:

Wash the pork with lime juice and water or you can use vinegar and water. Make sure you wash it again twice with just plain water. Add scotch bonnet peppers, scallion, thyme, allspice, garlic, onions, splenda, salt, black pepper, cinnamon, nutmeg, ginger, olive oil, soy sauce, lime juice, vinegar, liquid smoke, ½ cup water and ketchup to a blender or food processor. Pulse for 30 seconds; you want the mixture (jerk rub) to be a smooth consistency. Once the mixture (jerk rub) is done pulsing. Pour it on top of the pork and work it through each piece of meat with your hands. Make sure everything is evenly distributed. Now add the browning, it helps the meat to develop a brown color but browning does have some added sugar and carbs. So you don't have to use it. In the photo above I added more browning then this recipe calls for. So your pork may not come out as dark as mine. Let the jerk rub marinade overnight or for at least 2 hours. Cover the meat with plastic wrap and place it in the fridge. Preheat the oven to 375. Place the pork on a large roasting pan or whatever you have that you use to roast meat in. Add ½ cup of water to the pan. Let it roast for 2 to 3 hours depending in your oven with foil paper on top of the roasting pan. Every 20 minutes or so; you should check the meat to see if you need to add more water as the water dissolves. You will know the pork is ready, when you stick a fork in the meat and it is tender or the meat is falling off the bone a bit. At the last 15 minutes of baking the pork. Take the foil off, so the pork can get some color.

Approx. Nutritional Facts per Serving: *366.6 Calories, 29.4g Fat, 5.8g Net Carbs, 17.6g Protein*

Rasta Pasta

Yield: 10 Servings

Ingredients:

8oz. Chicken Breasts or more (Strips)

1 Bag Ciao Nutriwell Penne Pasta

1 ¼ Cup Heavy Cream

3 Tablespoons from Jerk Rub (store brought must be no more than 1g carb/you can use the jerk rub from the jerk pork recipe)

¼ Teaspoon Salt (Optional)

½ Medium Green Bell Peppers (Julienne)

½ Medium Yellow Bell Peppers (Julienne)

½ Medium Red Bell Peppers (Julienne)

1 Packet Knorr Parma Mix

¼ Cup Parmesan Cheese (optional)

1 Tablespoon Butter

Instructions:

If you haven`t cooked the chicken yet. Cut the chicken into medium size strips. Marinate it in jerk seasoning. You can either bake or fry the chicken. Set the chicken to the side. Turn your stove on medium heat. Add three cups of water to a pot. Bring it to a boil, then add the pasta and allow it to boil until it is al dente. The best way to test if it is al dente is to taste one of the noodles. It should take anywhere from 8 to 10 minutes. Strain the pasta in strainer. In a separate pan add the butter and put it on the stove at medium heat. Allow it to melt a bit and then add the heavy cream. With a big spoon, keep stirring the heavy cream. As it starts to thicken, add in the knorr parma mix. Keep stirring.Then add in the parmesan cheese and pasta. With your big spoon begin mixing the cheese into the pasta. At this point taste the pasta. If you feel it needs salt. Add the salt. I personally don`t think it needs salt but if you do. Feel free to use it. Then add the chicken. Stir everything together to make sure it is evenly distributed. Then add the peppers at the last minute of cooking. You don't want the peppers to be soft. They should be crunchy; if you want them somewhat soft. Then cook this for a couple minutes; with the lid on. Add a little bit of water if you're going to cook the peppers for longer. So they don't burn.

Approx. Nutritional Facts per Serving: *220.0 Calories, 13.8g Fat, 10.1g Net Carbs, 14.2g Protein*

Escovitch Fish

Yield: 8 Servings

Ingredients:

4 Whole Snapper Fish

1 Teaspoon Salt

1 Teaspoon Black Pepper

2 Cups Oil

Escovitch Dressing:

½ Whole Green Bell Pepper (Julienne)

½ Whole Red Bell Pepper (Julienne)

½ Medium Onion (Julienne)

½ Medium Carrot (Julienne)

3 Tablespoons Olive Oil

¾ Cup Vinegar

6 Pimento Seeds

½ Teaspoon Salt

1 Scotch Bonnet Pepper, seeds removed and Chopped Finely

Paper Towels

Instructions:

If you don't eat the fish head; then remove it and discard it. Clean and scale the fish. Make sure you throw away the blood and guts. Soak the fish in vinegar or lime mixed with water. Then wash it again twice with just water. Then cut the fish in half. Season the fish with salt and black pepper. Make sure you rub the seasoning in the fish very well. Turn the stove on medium high heat and add the oil. Allow the oil to get hot and then place the fish in. Pat fry the fish for 5 minutes on each side (the fish should have a golden brown color). Take the fish out of the oil and set it on paper towels. In a large bowl add vinegar, carrots, pimento seeds, peppers, onions, scotch bonnet pepper, oil and salt. Mix everything together with a big spoon. Then remove the fish from the paper towel onto a big platter. Pour the vinegar mixture on top of the fish.

Approx. Nutritional Facts per Serving: *214.6 Calories, 12.0g Fat, g Net Carbs, 22.8g Protein*

Stuffed Fish

Yield: 4 Servings

Ingredients:

4 Red Snapper Fish

2 Tablespoons Jerk Rub (Use recipe from jerk pork/or store bought brand with less than 1g Carbs)

4 Tablespoons Butter

1 Cup Onion Chopped

4 Cups Spinach

1 Teaspoon Salt

¼ Teaspoon Black Pepper

1 Teaspoon Garlic Powder

2oz. Shrimp (cooked)

8 Sprigs Thyme

4 Foil Paper

Instructions:

Preheat oven to 375F. Follow the same instructions for "Escovitch Fish" when it comes to cleaning and scaling the fish. Pat dry the fish. Begin seasoning the fish with salt, black pepper, garlic powder and jerk seasoning. Open the inside of the fish and stuff with 1 cup of spinach each, some shrimp, thyme, onion and butter. Place the fish on the foil paper and begin covering the entire fish in the foil paper. It does not need to be covered too tight. Place in the oven for 20 minutes.

Approx. Nutritional Facts per Serving: *197.1Calories, 7.7g Fat, 2.8g Net Carbs, 26.8g Protein*

Beef Patties

Yield: About 6-7 Patties

Ingredients (Crust):

2 Cup Dixie Diner Carb Counter Low Carb Flour

6 Tablespoons Psyllium Husk

1 Stick of Butter

2 Teaspoon Curry Powder

½ to 1 Teaspoon Salt

1 Teaspoon Splenda

½ Teaspoon Baking Powder

½ Cup Ice Cold Water

Ingredients (Filling):

4 to 6 oz Ground Beef

1 Medium Onion Chopped

4 Garlic Cloves Chopped

1 Scotch Bonnet Pepper

1 Tablespoon Dried Thyme

1 Tablespoon Allspice

½ Tablespoon Salt

1 Teaspoon Black Pepper

2 Tablespoons Splenda

1 Tablespoon Sugar Free Ketchup

Instructions:

This step is very important when it comes to the ground beef. If you decide not to blend the following ingredients in a food processor or blender; you risk the finely ground texture of the meat and flavor. Please do not skip this step. Begin by adding the chopped onion, garlic cloves, scotch bonnet pepper, thyme, allspice, salt, black pepper, splenda and ketchup to your food processor or blender. Pulse/ blend all the ingredients until it is a smooth consistency. Pour the mixture on the beef and begin combining and mixing everything together, so it is evenly distributed throughout the meat. You can place this in the fridge to marinate for an hour if you like or set to the side while you make the flour. In a medium size bowl, add the flour, psyllium husk, butter, curry powder, salt, splenda and baking powder. Mix everything together with a fork. Then, pour the water in slowly and with your hands start working and combining the flour until it is one big ball. It should be a slightly sticky dough. Wrap the dough in a plastic wrap and store it in the fridge for an hour. Turn your stove on medium heat. Add one tablespoon olive oil to your pan. Allow the oil to get hot and pour in your ground beef. Stir the meat with a big spoon and let this cook for 10 to 15 minutes. Throughout the cooking process, use your spoon to break down the meat so it has a nice fine consistency. Then cover the pan with a lid for another 5 to 10 minutes. There should be very little gravy in the pan. You need the least amount of gravy as possible. Too much gravy will make the patties messy and they won't come out right. Once the meat is cooked; turn the stove off and let the meat cool. You want the meat to be a cool temperature because if it is too hot. It will melt through the flour and ruin everything. Take the dough out of the fridge. Break off about 6-7 pieces of the dough. Roll or flatten each piece of dough until it forms a shape similar to a circle. Place about two tablespoon of the beef in the center of the dough. Grab one end of the dough and fold it over the other side. So it`s completely covered. You can take your fork and at the end of the patties create little lines on the side. But make sure, you seal the ends of the patties with your fingers. So nothing comes out. Repeat these steps for each patty. Place each patty on parchment paper. Bake in the oven for 20-30 minutes at 375. If you have left over ground beef, you can store it in the freezer to use at a later time.

Approx. Nutritional Facts per Servings: *305.9 Calories, 18.7g Fat, 7.2g Net Carbs, 18.2g Protein*

Curry Crab Legs

Ingredients:

2 Pounds Steamed Crab Legs

1 Can Coconut Milk

1 Cup Tomatoes (Chopped)

1 Scotch bonnet Pepper (Remove seeds)

3 Tablespoons Curry Powder

1 Teaspoon Salt (You may need more or less depending on how much salt is in the broth you choose)

¼ Teaspoon Black Pepper

4 Garlic Cloves (Chopped)

2 Scallions

2 Cups Water

1 Tablespoon Allspice

1 Tablespoon Dried Thyme

1 ½ Tablespoon Splenda

½ Cup Vegetable Broth

4 Ginger Root Slices

1 Tablespoon Coconut Oil

Instructions:

Turn your stove on medium heat. Add the coconut oil to the pan. Then in a cup add the coconut milk and curry powder, mix them together and add it to the pan. Then add the tomatoes, salt, black pepper, garlic, allspice, ginger, thyme, vegetable broth, splenda and water. Let this cook for 10 minutes. Cover the pot slightly. Then add scotch bonnet pepper and scallion. Mix everything together. Let it cook for another 15 to 20 minutes. Every couple of minutes, you should stir the pot with a big spoon. The gravy should be thick. If it isn't thick, cook it a little longer. Then add the crab legs and mix everything. Cook for 5 minutes.

Approx. Nutritional Facts per Serving: *220.1 Calories, 11.5g Fat, 10.7g Net Carbs, 6.6g Protein*

Curry Chicken

Yield: 8 Servings

Ingredients:

1 Whole Chicken or more cut up in very small pieces (skin removed)

3 Tablespoons Curry Powder (depending on the brand you use, you may need more)

3 Cups Water

1 Tablespoon Coconut Oil

1 Teaspoon Allspice

1/2 Tablespoon Salt

1 Teaspoon Black Pepper

Some Sprig thyme

1 Scotch Bonnet Pepper (Remove seeds)

2 Scallions

2 Tablespoons Ketchup

1 Medium Onion (Chopped)

½ Medium Green Bell Peppers (Chopped)

4 Garlic Cloves (Chopped)

1 Can Coconut Milk

1 Tablespoon Poultry Seasoning (No Added Carbs)

1 Sazon Seasoning Packet (No Salt Added)

Instructions:

Wash the chicken and pat dry. In a large bowl, add the chicken. Pour the curry powder, allspice, salt, black pepper, scotch bonnet peppers, onions, garlic, bell peppers, thyme, ketchup, sazon, scallion and poultry seasoning. Use your hands to rub the ingredients into the chicken. Make sure you coat every piece of chicken. Place a plastic wrap over the bowl and place it in the fridge overnight. When you're ready to cook the chicken; turn the stove on medium heat, add the coconut oil. Allow it to melt a bit and then add the chicken in along with 3 cups of water. Cover the pot with a lid but leave it slightly uncovered. Cook this for 30 minutes, every 10 minute. Check on the chicken to see if you need more water. If it needs more add a cup of water. After 30 minutes, add the coconut milk. Let this cook for another 30 minutes. Again, check on the meat every 10 minutes to make sure you don't need any more water. By this point, you shouldn't need more water but if you do. Add more.

Approx. Nutritional Facts per Serving: *131 Calories, 7.3g Fat, 6.8g Net Carbs, 6.1g Net Carbs*

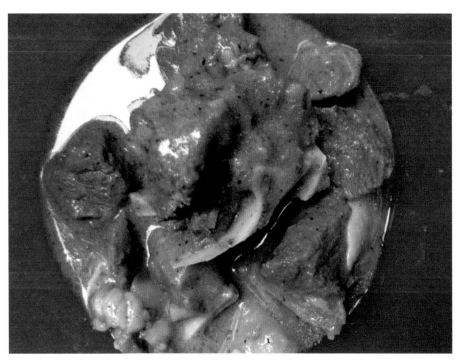

Curry Goat

Yield: 8 Servings

Ingredients:

2 Pounds Goat Meat

4 Tablespoons Curry Powder

1 Tablespoon Black Pepper

1/2 Tablespoon Salt

1 Medium Onion (Chopped)

1 Scotch Bonnet Pepper (Chopped)

4 Garlic Cloves Mashed

1 Can Coconut Milk

2 Tablespoons Dried Thyme

1 Medium Green Bell Pepper (Chopped)

2 Scallions

2 Tablespoons Coconut Oil

1 Tablespoon Allspice

1 Tablespoon Sugar free Ketchup

5 or More Cups Water

Instructions:

Wash the goat meat. In a large bowl, add the meat and the ingredients (except the coconut oil, water and coconut milk) together. Using both hands, rub the seasoning into the meat. Making sure everything is evenly distributed. Cover with a plastic wrap and let it marinate overnight; when you're ready to cook the goat meat. Turn the stove on medium heat. Add the coconut oil to your pot. Allow it to melt a bit and then add the meat to the pot. Allow it to cook for 5 minutes and then add 5 cups of water. Cover with the pot`s lid (slightly). Cook for 2 hours; every 20 to 30 minutes, check the meat to see if you need to add more water. If you do, add only a little bit of water at a time because you're going to add the coconut milk later. After 2 hours, add the coconut milk and cook for another 1 to 2 hours. Mix everything with a big spoon. Turn down the heat a bit. Continue to check on it every 20 minutes.

Approx. Nutritional Facts per Serving: *187.6 Calories, 7.6g Fat, 4.3g Net Carbs, 24.1g Protein*

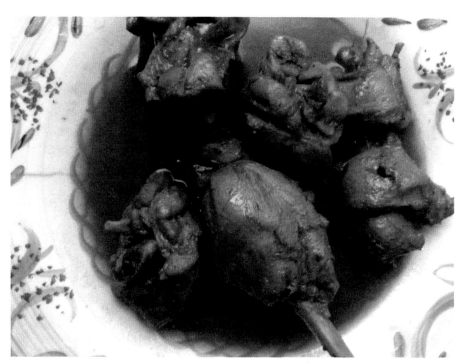

Brown Stew Chicken

Yield: 8-10 Servings

Ingredients:

1 Whole Chicken or more cut up in very small pieces (skinless)

½ Tablespoon Salt

1 Teaspoon Black Pepper

1 Tablespoon Poultry Seasoning

1 Tablespoon Allspice

1 Tablespoon Garlic Powder

1 Cup Onion (Chopped)

3 Scallions

2 Ginger Slices

1 Tablespoon Dried Thyme

3 Cups Olive Oil

¼ Cup Soy Sauce or 2 to 3 Tablespoons Browning

2 Tablespoons Sugar Free Ketchup

2 Tablespoons Splenda

3 to 4 Cups Water

Instructions:

Wash the chicken and pat it dry. Place the chicken in a large bowl. Add the salt, black pepper, poultry seasoning, allspice, garlic powder, thyme, soy sauce and ketchup. If you decide to use soy sauce, you may want to adjust how much salt you use because soy sauce has salt in it. So maybe you may need less salt. It never hurts to only add one teaspoon of salt at first and if you need more. You can always add it in later. If you use browning, then one tablespoon of salt is needed. Once you decide if you are going to use soy sauce or browning. Allow the chicken to marinate in the seasoning overnight. Then turn the stove on medium high heat, add the oil to the pan. Allow it to get hot; it should take 5 to 7 minutes. Take each piece of chicken and place it in the oil. You want to fry the pieces on each side for about 5 minutes, so it develops a golden brown color on each side. When you are done frying each piece; take them out the pan and place them in a bowl. Throw the oil away but leave about a tablespoon of the oil in the pan. Turn down the heat to medium low; add the chicken back in along with the onions, scallion, ginger, splenda and water. Cover the pan, leave the lid slightly uncovered. Cook for 45 minutes. Every 10 to 15 minutes, check to see if the chicken needs more water.

Approx. Nutritional Facts per Serving: *184.5 Calories, 16.2g Fat, 4.8g Net Carbs, 4.4g Protein*

Oxtails

Yield: 8 Servings

Ingredients:

2 Pounds Oxtails

2 Tablespoons Coconut Oil

1 Teaspoon Black Pepper

1/2 Tablespoon Salt

2 Cups Onion (Chopped)

1 Green Bell Pepper (Chopped)

4 Garlic Cloves (Chopped)

4 Scallions (Chopped)

2 Tablespoons Dried Thyme

3 Tablespoons Sugar Free Ketchup

3 Tablespoons Splenda

1 Tablespoon Allspice

4 Ginger Root

½ Cup Carrots (Chopped/Optional)

6 Cups Water

1 Can Butter beans (Optional/From the can)

2- 3 Tablespoons Browning (No more than 4g Carbs)

Blender or food Processor

Scotch Bonnet Pepper (Chopped)

Instructions:

Wash the oxtails; then put them in a large bowl. Add the browning, black pepper, onions, bell pepper, garlic, thyme, ketchup, splenda, allspice, ginger, and salt to either your food processor or blender. Mix everything until it is a smooth and thick consistency. Then pour the mixture on the oxtails. At this time add the browning as well. Using your hands; mix and rub everything evenly throughout every single piece of meat. Cover it with a plastic wrap. Place it in the fridge overnight; when you are ready to cook the oxtails. Turn the stove on medium heat, add the coconut oil to the pot and allow it to melt a bit. Then add the meat and one cup of water. Allow that to cook for 10 minutes. Then add the last 5 cups of water, scallion and cover the pot with the lid (slightly). Let this cook for 3 hours. Every 20 to 30 minutes. Check on the meat to see if it needs more water. You're going to need a good amount of water for this recipe because oxtails is very tough and it takes some time to soften. You may also need to turn down the heat a bit as well. If you have a pressure cooker it will cook much faster. If you need to add more water, add more. After three hours, add in the butter beans (from the can) and carrots. I don`t usually cook oxtails with beans and carrots because I like to make this stew as low in carbs as possible but the choice is yours. Continue to cook this for another 15 to 20 minutes. You will know the meat is ready, when you stick a fork in the meat and it is soft and tender. Another indication is, the meat falling off the bone. Remove the scallion when you're ready to serve the meat.

Approx. Nutritional Facts per Serving (No Carrots or Butter Beans Included): *423.4 Calories, 34.2gFat, 7.0g Net Carbs, 21.7g Protein*

Pelau Chicken

Yield: 8 Servings

Ingredients:

6 Boneless Chicken thigh (skinless) cut in small pieces

1 Teaspoon Black Pepper

1/2 Tablespoon Salt

¼ Cup Soy Sauce

1 Teaspoon Worcestershire Sauce

1 Tablespoon Sugar Free Ketchup

4 Garlic Cloves

4 Ginger Root Slices

1 Cup Onion (Chopped)

½ Cup Tomatoes (Chopped)

3 Tablespoons Splenda

1 Jalapeno Pepper (Remove Seeds/Chopped)

1 Tablespoon Dried Cilantro

2 Sprigs Thyme

¼ Cup Coconut Milk

1 Cup Pigeon Peas (beans) it can be either the green or brown/canned

3 Cups Cauliflower Rice (following cauliflower recipe)

¼ Cup Chicken Broth

2 Eggs scrambled (optional)

2 Scallions (Chopped)

2 Tablespoons Coconut Oil

1 Cup Pumpkin (Chopped)

Food Processor

Instructions:

Begin by washing your chicken. Turn your stove on medium heat. Add the coconut oil to your pot, allow the coconut oil to melt a bit and add in the chicken, Worcestershire sauce and soy sauce. Let this cook for 15 minutes. Turn down the stove a bit so the chicken does not burn. Then add in the eggs to the side of the pan and with a big spoon begin to scramble them. Once that is done; mix the chicken and eggs together. Add in the black pepper, salt, ketchup, garlic, ginger, onions, tomatoes, splenda, jalapeno, dried cilantro, thyme, pigeon peas, scallion, chicken broth, coconut milk and pumpkin. Cover the pot and allow it to cook for another 15 minutes. At this point place the cauliflower rice in the microwave for 6 minutes and then take it out the microwave and set it to the side. Then add in the cauliflower rice to the pan. Mix everything together with a big spoon. Cook for 5 minutes. You don't want the cauliflower to get too mushy. When you're ready to serve, remove the Scallion and sprig thyme.

Approx. Nutritional Facts per Serving: *160.2 Calories, 7.8g Fat, 9.4g Net Carbs, 10.9g Protein*

Pepperpot

Yield: 8 – 10 Serving

Ingredients:

1 Pound Beef Chunks/ Cut for Stew

1 ½ Pound Oxtails

1 Pound Cow foot (Optional but traditional)

2 Tablespoons Olive Oil

1 Scotch Bonnet Pepper (Chopped)

1 Tablespoon Ground Clove

½ Cup Splenda

2 Tablespoons Thyme

1 Tablespoon Cinnamon

½ Tablespoon Salt

1 Teaspoon Black Pepper

1 Medium Onion (Chopped)

4 Garlic Cloves Mashed

2 Tablespoons Cassareep

1 Orange Peel

Large Size Pot/Medium Size Pot

About 11 ½ to 12 Cups Water

Fact:

While writing this book I learned that Guyana is technically not geographically located in the Caribbean but it is still considered a part of the Caribbean. Either way I'm paying respect to them with this popular recipe "Pepperpot"; it is normally made with a cup of cassareep but cassareep is a mixture of Cassava and sugar together. Since we are eating low carb, that is too much carbs and sugar. But they do have brands that use the cassava extract instead of the real thing. That saves a lot of carbs. I still couldn't find a brand that has less than 6g of sugar though. Please understand it is the cassareep that gives the pepperpot that delicious flavor. So before you start saying you will just do this recipe without it. You may want to reconsider; if you can afford the extra carbs and sugar. Give it a try. Just keep in mind because we are not using the normal amount of cassareep (1cup or more). Our pepperpot won't have the dark brown color is usually has. At first glance this can be mistaken for regular stew oxtails. Based on the dish's appearance. I didn't include cowfoot in this recipe but feel free to try it.

Instructions:

Begin by washing your meat. You will need two pots (one needs to be a large pot). Turn the stove on medium heat. In your large pot, add one tablespoon of olive oil. Allow the pot to get hot. Add in the oxtails and with a big spoon. Keep stirring and flipping the meat on each side. So it develops a brown color. Keep doing this for about 5 minutes or so. Then add 5 cups of water and cover the pot with a lid. Let the oxtails cook for 3 hours until they start to soften. Make sure to check on the meat to see if it needs more water; you don't want it to burn. Then at the last 30 minutes of the oxtails cooking. In a smaller pot on medium heat, add the other tablespoon of olive oil. At this point, you're going to add the beef and with a big spoon. Flip the pieces of meat on both sides. So it develops some color. Add two cups of water and bring it to a boil for 30 minutes. Then add the beef to the pot that has the oxtails in it. Add some ground cloves, splenda, thyme, cinnamon, salt, black pepper, onions, scotch bonnet pepper, orange peel, garlic and cassareep. With your big spoon, stir everything together. Cook for another 45 minutes. Every 20 minutes, you should check the meat again to see if it needs anymore water. If it does add in more water.

Approx. Nutritional Facts per Serving: *366.5 Calories, 29.8g Fat, 3.8g Net Carbs, 20.3g Protein*

Guyanese Style Lo Mein

Yield: 6 Servings

Ingredients:

½ Bag Asian Explore Organic Soybean Spaghetti

½ Pound Shrimp (Cooked)

2 Cups Green Cabbage (Optional)

1 Medium Onion (Chopped)

4 Garlic Cloves

2 Scallions

1 Chili Pepper (Chopped)

½ Green Bell Peppers

½ Red Bell Peppers

½ Yellow Bell Peppers

1 Cup Broccoli

1 Cup Celery (Chopped/Optional)

1 Teaspoon Salt

½ Teaspoon Black Pepper

2 Tablespoons Coconut Oil

1 Teaspoon Sesame Oil

1 Tablespoon Hoisin Sauce (It is a bit high in carbs so find the one with the less amount of carbs)

1 Tablespoon Oyster Sauce

1 Tablespoon Soy Sauce

Wok

Instructions:

Turn your stove on high heat; add 5 cups of water to a pot. As the water starts to boil, add the pasta noodles. These noodles are kind of tricky because their softer than regular noodles when cooked. So you don't want them to boil for too long. 6 minutes should be good enough, take one noodle out after the 6 minutes are up. If it's soft enough then take the pot off the stove and strain the water out of the noodles with a strainer. Set the noodles aside. Turn the stove down to medium heat and add the coconut oil to the wok. Then add the garlic and the soy sauce and let that cook for 15 minutes. If you need to add a little water to stop this from burning, then do so. Add in the cooked shrimp, green cabbage, onions, scallion, chili pepper, bell peppers, broccoli, celery, salt, black pepper, sesame oil, oyster sauce and hoisin sauce. Mix everything together with a big spoon. Let this cook for another 5 - 8 minutes. Then add in the pasta and mix everything together again with your big spoon. Cook for 3 minutes.

Approx. Nutritional Facts per Servings(Cabbage Included): *237.8 Calories, 8.1g Fat, 11.3g Net Carbs, 22.3g Protein*

Griot (Fried Pork)

Yield: 8 Servings

Ingredients:

2 Pound Pork shoulder (cut in small chunks)

½ Medium Onion Chopped

1 Scotch Bonnet Pepper Chopped

4 Garlic Cloves Crushed

2 Tablespoons Dried Thyme

1 Tablespoon Salt

1/2 Teaspoon Black Pepper

The Juice of 2 Limes

1 Teaspoon Adobo Seasoning (Low Sodium)

1 Sazon Packet (Optional/ No Salt Added)

1 Tablespoon Dried Parsley

About 2- 4 Cups Water

½ Cup Green Bell Peppers

4 Cups Canola Oil

Roasting Pan

Instructions:

Wash the pork, and pat dry. Place the pork in a bowl with all the ingredients except the oil and water. Let this marinate for 30 minutes. Then set your oven on 400, place the pork in a roasting pan with ½ cup of water and allow it to roast for 1 ½ hours. It is a good idea to place foil paper over the roasting pan. You should check on the meat every 20 minutes or so. To see if it needs more water to prevent burning and the meat sticking to the pan. Then take the pork out. Turn the stove on medium high heat, in a pot add the oil and allow this to heat up. Then add just the pork pieces to the oil, try your best not to get the juices from the pan in the oil. Don't add too many pieces at once to the oil. You just want the pork to fry a bit and develop a golden brown color. Fry each piece for about 3 to 5 minutes. Place on paper towel. Remove the pork from the paper towel and add it to a platter, you can pour the juices from the roasting pan on top of the pork.

Approx. Nutritional Facts per Serving: *240.6 Calories, 18.4g Fat, 2.1g Net Carbs, 15.5g Protein*

Bully Beef and Cabbage (Also Known As Corn Beef and Cabbage)

Yield: 6 Servings

Ingredients:

2 Cups Shredded Cabbage

1 Cup Onion (Chopped)

1 Cup Tomatoes Diced

1 Scotch Bonnet Pepper (Chopped)

¼ Teaspoon Black Pepper

1 Can Bully Beef (corn beef in a tin can)

2 Tablespoon Sugar Free Ketchup

1 Tablespoon Olive Oil

Instructions:

Turn your stove on medium low heat. Add the olive oil to your pan. Allow the oil to heat up, and then add the tomatoes and onions. Allow that to cook for 5 minutes. Then add the scotch bonnet pepper. At this time you want to twist the key of the corn beef can, once it is open. Grab a big spoon and pour out the beef on to the pan with the oil, scotch bonnet pepper, onions and tomatoes. Using that same spoon, break the meat up in small pieces. Until it is a smooth consistency; kind of like ground beef that has been processed through a food processor. Then add the ketchup and black pepper. At this point add in the cabbage as well. Mix everything together with your big spoon. So everything is evenly distributed. Cover the pot with a lid slightly for 5 to 10 minutes. Add ¼ cup of water if you see the meat starting to stick to the pot. Take off the lid; cook until the cabbage is soft. The best way to test if the cabbage is soft; is to actually taste it.

Approx. Nutritional Facts per Serving: *101.0 Calories, 5.6g Fat, 3.9g Net Carbs, 7.5g Protein*

It looks like we are at the end of my book. I want to thank you one more time for purchasing this book. If you didn't find a Caribbean recipe that you may have eaten before and wanted to try it. Don`t worry because I am writing a Part 2 to this book as we speak. That book will be available in 2015. It will feature more Caribbean Recipes but it will focus more on Islands in the Caribbean that I didn't touch on in this book. Please don't be afraid to contact me with any concerns or questions you may have. My contact information is listed at the beginning of this book if you missed it.

About The Author

Kayanna D. Jennings was born on November 25, 1989 in Brooklyn, New York to a Jamaican mother of Chinese Indian descent and an Afro- Jamaican father who has white ancestry. As a child Kayanna was always known as being shy, quiet and timid. This had a lot to do with the teasing she endured as a child for being overweight. As she got older she reached her highest weight of 247 pounds and decided at 19 years old. She had to do something about it. She followed a low carb diet and workout regime. This resulted in her losing over 60+ pounds in 3 to 4 months. She kept the weight off for three years until she faced some personal issues. She does not fully blame her personal issues for her weight gain. But she admits it had more to do with not fully educating herself once she became low carb. She was under the impression at that time (like many others) that eating low carb meant she couldn't enjoy all the food she grew up eating and loved. She later realized and learned a lot of the food she grew up eating in her Caribbean household happens to be low in carbs. She also realized that the dishes she enjoyed as a child that were high in carbs. Were still an option for her as long as she modified them the low carb way. Once she stumbled upon this discovery. She became excited about being a low carber and wrote her first book "My Low Carb Journal and her second book "My Low Carb Caribbean Cuisine". She also created her own website as a platform to develop a closer relationship with her fellow low carbers. She believes that just because you eat low carb does not mean you cannot enjoy things that are not considered low carb on occasions. She has been quoted as saying "If I want bread, I'll make bread out of almond flour, if I want pasta, I'll enjoy a bowl of miracle noodles and if I want Coldstone ice cream. I`ll enjoy that as well but in moderation".Kayanna`s goal is to teach others, *"Low Carb is not a diet, but a lifestyle"*.

Made in the USA
Monee, IL
12 September 2021

MY LOW CARB CARIBBEAN CUISINE

ISBN 9781502814067

LPN

Roads Once Traveled
(In the Hills of the Blue Ridge)

By H Wayne Easter